The Savvy Seller

*How to Sell Your Home
for Top Dollar with Great Terms
in the Shortest Time Possible*

By
Krista Mashore

Realtor®
Lic #01346304
Broker Associate
01513330

Savvy Sellers: *How to Sell Your Home for Top Dollar with Great Terms in the Shortest Time Possible*

How to get the highest price and best terms from the sale of your home

© 2020 **Krista Mashore**

All rights reserved. No part of this book may be used or reproduced in any manner whatsoever without prior written consent of the authors, except as provided by the United States of America copyright law.

Published by Krista Mashore, Brentwood, CA

ISBN: 978-0-9990828-4-3 paperback

This publication is designed to provide accurate and authoritative information with regard to the subject matter covered. It is sold with the understanding that the author is not engaged in rendering legal, accounting, or other professional advice. If legal advice or other expert assistance is required, the services of a competent professional should be sought.

For more information, please write: Homes By Krista
7620 Balfour Road, Brentwood, California, USA 94513

Visit us online at: www.KristaHomes.com

The Mashore Manifesto

I am a Community Market Leader. I am not just a Real Estate Agent, I am an **UNSTOPPABLE** visionary! I am **REVOLUTIONIZING** the practice of real estate and **CONTRADICTING** the old school teaching method and approach. I am a **LIFE LONG** learner.

I **SERVE**, I do not just sell! I strive for excellence for myself and my clients. I am changing the way Real Estate is being done and how agents are looked at. I don't rely on traditional measures of getting clients and generating leads. I focus on the **FUTURE**!

I continue to push because I know that nothing happens overnight. I appreciate overwhelm because it means that I am **GROWING**. I **PUSH** and give my **ALL**. I will **NEVER GIVE UP!**

I have an **ABUNDANCE** mindset! I know that I am the **ONLY ONE** responsible for **CREATING** the life that I **DESERVE**, and I **AM!**

I AM:

A MARKETER
ABUNDANT
SUCCESSFUL
HELPFUL
ORIGINAL
RESOURCEFUL
AN EDUCATOR

I am a
COMMUNITY MARKET LEADER!

Praise for Krista & Her Team

My father in law passed and we needed to sell his house. We met with three different agents and we quickly decided to go with Krista. Krista and her team are very knowledgeable, energetic and at the top of their game. The strategy, marketing and pricing on the house were spot on. They were very good at communicating and walking us through every step of the process. It was quite easy and painless.

—Shawn & Heather Burns

The Krista Mashore team was awesome! We were so impressed with their marketing techniques! They sure know how to sell a home in this age of social media. Their team was very professional from staging, to marketing, to closing. They kept us updated and made sure we had a successful and timely closing.

—Yolanda and Doug

I can't speak more highly of the Mashore Group! They were always available to answer our questions and give us guidance as we maneuvered through selling our home. The staging that they did on our home was invaluable and the photos were excellent. I feel that their technology was definitely ahead of most realtors and helped get eyes on our property. It was like working with a trusted knowledgeable friend.

—Cindy Crowe

We started the selling process months earlier with another local agent that assured us he knew the market and priced our home to sell. We agonized for three months and had only two showings. We canceled the listing and switched to Homes by Krista. We had multiple showings and a full price offer within a month. This company KNOWS what it takes to get the job done.

—ME Klekar

MEET KRISTA

As one of the top 1% of realtors nationwide, Krista Mashore has sold over 2,000 homes since entering the field in 2001. She is known throughout East County in California as the Digital Marketing Queen. As the Broker/Owner of Homes by Krista, she has put together an unbeatable team whose primary focus and goal is happy clients with highly successful outcomes. Homes by Krista, which includes a digital marketer and marketing specialist, markets each client's home like a multi-million-dollar home regardless of the listed selling price. Every property receives basic staging, digital marketing platform, professional photography, videography, drone photography, as well as property-specific websites, four-page color brochures, virtual reality tours, and so much more!(If you'd like to learn more about Krista's Strategic Digital Marketing Plan, which gets homes in front of hundreds of thousands of eyes, go to www.SellSavvyNow.com)

Author of five books, Krista now runs a national training program coaching real estate agents in cutting-edge best practices in the industry. Krista's ultimate goal is to help clients, her fellow agents, and her community in any way she can. One of Krista's favorite projects is coaching teens in her community through her non-profit, *Teens Lifting Lives*.

Krista lives with her awesome husband, Steve, her amazing children, Jaynlin, Kayli, and Casey, and her adorable French Bulldog, Pepper, in Brentwood, California.

Krista's Credentials and Awards:

Education:

Master of Arts M.A.

Bachelor of Science B.S.

Elementary School Credentialed Teacher

Awards:

Wall Street Journal Real Trends Top 1% Nationally

Top 1% in Units and Production in California

2 Comma Club

America's Top 100

Expert Network Distinguished Realtors

Credentials:

GRI (Graduate Realtor™ Institute)

CRS (Council of Residential Specialists)

MCNE (Master Certified Negotiation Expert)

CNE (Certified Negotiation Expert)
ILHM (Institute for Luxury Home Marketing)
e-Pro (Technology Designation)
Real Estate Divorce Specialist
BPOR (Broker Price Options Resource)
Advanced Evaluations
Equator and RES NET Certified
CHS (HAFA Certified) CDPE (Certified Distressed Properties Expert)
Five Star Short Sale Certified

If I can answer any questions or offer assistance, please feel free to contact me at 925-325-HOME (4663). And be sure to go to www.SellSavvyNow.com for informational videos that are full of valuable information. We can also get you a Free Marketing Analysis and a Home Evaluation.

Contents

Meet Krista	vi
Introduction	1
Choosing a Savvy Listing Agent	4
Credentials	6
Experience	7
Reputation	9
Overall Team	10
Outside Resources	11
Rapport	12
Savvy Seller Questions to Ask	13
Savvy Marketing in Today's World	16
Savvy Digital Marketing Power	18
Traditional Marketing on Steroids	21
Savvy Seller Questions to Ask	26

Contents

Savvy Negotiating for the Win — 28
- The Competitive Negotiator — 29
- The Compliant Negotiator — 30
- The Collaborative Negotiator — 32
- Your Job During Negotiations — 33
- Savvy Seller Questions to Ask — 35

Savvy Communication is Key — 37
- Starting Off on the Right Foot — 39
- Communication During the Marketing Stage — 43
- During Negotiation — 44
- During Escrow — 45
- Savvy Seller Questions to Ask — 47

Create Savvy Seller Goals and Priorities — 48
- Get Clarity — 50
- Clarity for Couples — 51
- Get Your Priorities Straight — 52
- Savvy Seller Questions to Ask — 55

Savvy Seller's Prep For A Great Sale — 57
- Set Up Your Home to Inspire Offers — 57
- Breeze Through Inspections — 62
- Major Repairs — 63

On the Market: Savvy Seller Do's and Don'ts — 65
- Showing Your Home — 65

A Last Word — 69

Social Media Analytics for Past Properties — 70

INTRODUCTION

Have you ever read the book, *What to Expect When You're Expecting*? It was written for couples expecting a baby, especially their first. It runs through all the physical ins and outs of pregnancy as well as the emotional roller coaster pregnancy puts you on. It talks about the people who will team up with you during the pregnancy, specifically what their role is, and what to expect from them. It explains things you, as a couple, can do to make the birth healthier and easier. Basically, it instructs you and warns you about a bunch of things so that you don't freak out!

Think of this book as, *What to Expect When You're Selling.* Yes, selling your home can be as emotional, joyful, scary, exciting and irritating as pregnancy! Unfortunately, too many sellers find themselves freaking out and not getting the happy, healthy end result they'd hoped for! In my experience, it does **not** have to be traumatic or a struggle. In fact, with the right team and the right information, the process can actually be fun and definitely successful.

I wrote this book to give you the information you need as a Seller to enjoy the ride and end up with the best result at "birth." As one of my fellow sellers, I want you to be *hugely* successful in the sale of your home!

In the first part of this book, I'll explain what you should look for in a listing agent and how to hire the one who will do the best job for you. You'll find out what you should expect every step of the way from a really good agent. It doesn't matter what price range your home falls into, I really want you to expect *superior* service from the listing agent you hire!

Later in the book, I'll talk about what *you* can do to be a strong partner with your agent, making the process easier and more successful. Decades ago, dads used to hang out in the waiting room, biting their nails, smoking, and worrying while their spouse did all the heavy lifting. Real estate used to be that way (and with some agents, it still is!). But your positive contribution to the entire process can make a huge difference to the final result. So, I'll give you some tips of things you can do *before* your house goes on the market, *while* it's being shown, and *during* the final negotiations and closing process.

My motto has always been: When You Do What You Love . . . People Love What You Do." And I LOVE selling homes and helping the people I work with!

If you have any questions after reading this book, feel free to contact me at 925-325-HOME (4663). And be sure to go to www.SellSavvyNow.com for informational videos that are easy to watch and full of valuable information. We

Introduction

can also get you a Free Marketing Analysis and a Home Evaluation of your home.

This book is my gift to you, along with my very best wishes for the successful sale of your home!

Krista Mashore

CHOOSING A SAVVY LISTING AGENT

One of the most important decisions you can make is in choosing the real estate team that will list your house. Unfortunately, many people just choose someone they know who happens to have a real estate license. While Uncle Harvey might be a super nice guy, he may *not* be the best agent to list and sell your property. Hiring someone who lacks experience can cost you thousands and thousands of dollars, even if he promises to give you the "family discount" and reduce his commission. First of all, he won't give you the high-octane marketing a real pro can give you. Second, mistakes and not knowing how to keep a transaction on track, especially when everything hits the fan, can be *extremely* costly in real estate. After selling over two thousand homes, I've witnessed every kind of misstep and screw up possible! And I've seen how horribly expensive they can be. Trying to save money on commissions by using someone inexperienced will cost you far more than the few percentages in commission you think you'll be saving. And I can't tell you how many times a seller has chosen a "discount broker" over me, only to come back to me months later when that agent couldn't get the job done!

It's like choosing a surgeon for a critical operation: You wouldn't just use your next-door neighbor to be your surgeon because he lends you his lawnmower and offers you a "family discount," right? Of course not! You would check his credentials, whether he specializes in the kind of surgery you need, his reputation, and a ton of other things before you'd let him slice into you!

Your home is a huge investment. So, even though it might hurt your uncle's or your neighbor's feelings, you need to choose the agent who will do the best job for you. Rather than just sitting through the dog and pony show of your first appointment with a prospective listing agent, use it as an in-depth interview. Don't be afraid to *grill them*.

The absolutely most critical parts of your listing agent's job are **marketing** and **negotiation**. If your Realtor® is not strong in understanding and implementing current best practices in *both* of those areas, they're doing you a disfavor to even take your listing! I am not kidding! Agents who are weak or "old school" will not be able to get you the best price and most favorable terms for your house even if they've been in the business for decades. They also won't be able to get the job done well, quickly, and without a lot of hassle.

Because these two areas—marketing and negotiations—are so very important, I'll be covering them in depth over the next chapters. You don't have to become an expert in either marketing or negotiation yourself. You just have to be very clear about the skills and services an agent *should* be offering you before you even think of signing on the dotted line with them. When you interview potential agents to list your house, you'll want to ask a ton of questions specific to marketing and negotiation.

Here's what else you should look for:

Credentials

Anyone can get a real estate license. A license doesn't necessarily mean they know what the heck they're doing. Agents who are really serious about the business join the National Association of Realtors® (NAR), which is real estate's national professional organization. (They'll have that designation on their business card.) Realtors® are required to follow the NAR's Code of Ethics and pass additional exams every two years that other agents don't.

All agents have basic continuing education requirements, but none of these courses do anything to help an agent learn best practices in selling homes. And to be quite honest, all of the education and credentials in the world will not take the place of experience. Experience is the only way to be the best of the best, to learn how to foresee and tackle problems before they arise, and to truly know the ins and outs of how to capitalize on the investment for the Seller. Those of us who strive for excellence in real estate have taken additional coursework to sharpen our skills or to learn more about our areas of specialty. We might have studied advanced negotiation, digital marketing, or trends in home financing. Courses like these often award a credential at successful completion.

Personally, I've got so many letters after my name that I can't even fit them all on my business card! I've got one designation, Master Certified Negotiation Expert (MCNE) that less than 0.1% of all real estate agents hold! Almost every agent in my office has their MCNE as well. I require it of them. The point isn't how *many* credentials and letters an agent has after their name. It matters *which* credentials they've chosen to go after, and it matters that they've taken the time to become the best they can be to become excellent at what they do and how they can serve you.

Don't hesitate to ask someone who wants to list your house about their credentials and additional education. And don't be impressed by fancy designations. Ask what they learned from their courses that will benefit you with the sale of your home.

Experience

Back to the surgeon analogy: Do you want a doctor who has successfully performed dozens of surgeries *exactly* like yours? Or do you want someone who typically works in a totally different specialty? Do you want someone who will be performing their very first surgery or someone who really knows their way around in the operating room?

Like many professions, good real estate agents typically specialize (or *should* specialize) in certain properties within a specific geographic area. We call it their "niche." Someone who tells you they can "sell anything anywhere" is just kidding themselves. They may be able to get the job done eventually, but they certainly won't know the best way to market your type of home—which means they will **not** get you the best result possible.

One the other hand, a listing agent who has sold dozens of homes like yours in your specific city or neighborhood will have the inside scoop and know what it will take to get you the best outcome. A really good and ethical agent, who does *not* deal with your type of property or isn't in your area, will refer you to someone else, or *at the very least,* partner with an agent who does specialize in that area and type of property.

What about years of experience? This can be a double-edged sword. If you've got someone with years of experience who is keeping up with current trends, social media and internet marketing, and who is a real go-getter, that's perfect! They bring you the wisdom of many transactions along with a cutting-edge process and twentieth century marketing.

But if you're considering someone with scads of experience who still does real estate the exact same way they did it when Reagan was in office, run for the hills! It's like hiring a surgeon who still sterilizes his scalpel over a hot flame! Real estate is so different than it was decades ago, even five years ago. The market has changed dramatically, and the way buyers search for and find homes is totally different. (Hint: It's online.) If your "experienced" agent doesn't know this, and doesn't know how to create an attractive landing page for your home, or get into the back end of Zillow to upgrade your home's profile and keep it in prime position, or how to create a strategic ad campaign on social media, well, you'd be shooting yourself in the foot to choose them.

You'd be much better off with a newbie who is gung-ho, tech savvy, smart, and knowledgeable about the market, marketing and digital marketing, and who is eager to do all they can to build themselves a great reputation. They'll treat you like gold because to them, you are! Just make sure that newbie is working for a good broker who will pay attention and guide them along the way.

Reputation

This is so important! You want someone who is respected in the community and who is *totally ethical* as your listing agent. In fact, why would you ever want to deal with someone who is unethical in *any* circumstance? Unless you're looking for a partner to help you rob a bank. But even then, you want the guy to be honest enough to give you your share of the loot, right?

No other agent or loan officer or escrow officer (or pizza delivery guy!) will want to work with an agent who is known to be shady or even extremely difficult to deal with. Why would another agent bring a deal from their really qualified buyers to an agent who is unresponsive, untrustworthy, and a pain in the you-know-what? Even if your home is the Taj Mahal and you're offering it at a screamin' great price, other agents will steer their clients as far away as possible. And if you *do* happen to enter into a Contract of Sale while Mr. or Ms. Shady-pants Agent has your listing, trust me, it will not go well. And in this litigious world we live in, you're putting yourself totally at risk.

Just don't hire that weasel! Plenty of professionals out there are ethical and respected. Don't invite unnecessary grief (and lawsuits!) by choosing the rotten apple in the barrel.

Okay, so how do you scope out an agent's reputation? Asking them for references would be nice but they'll only give you their most satisfied clients or the people they've bribed to say nice things. Your better bet is to go online and check out Google, Zillow, Facebook, Realtor.com, or Yelp for client reviews. You can also check with the Better Business Bureau and the Department of Real Estate. If you know some Realtors® in the area, ask if they have any insight into the agent you're considering.

Overall Team

It takes a village, right? Unless an agent is listing just one or maybe two houses at a time, they **cannot** keep on top of everything that needs to be done to get you the best result in the shortest amount of time! They need support. They need resources. They need other really committed, skilled, and talented people on their team to keep the momentum going during the sale of your home.

Not every great agent has an office of twenty staffers to run the show. Some professionals have built part-time teams or virtual teams that are highly efficient and effective. But if your prospective listing agent uses their pool maintenance guy to keep up their website and their thirteen-year old niece to design and mail out flyers, you need to look elsewhere.

A listing agent who strives for excellence will spend money to make sure their team is skilled, dedicated, and motivated. So much of what is done during the sale of your house will **not** be done by the agent who signs the listing agreement. It's important that you know who else will be working on your sale, what specifically they contribute, their experience, and how often you'll be interacting with them.

Outside Resources

Every transaction requires a number of outside resources: home inspectors, escrow officers, loan officers, insurance agents, even building and maintenance contractors. Realtors® who really know what they're doing have consciously cultivated a good team of these folks. They've vetted them, checked their work and their references, and probably work with them consistently. These are the professional experts your agent calls for advice and/or service.

Why do you care? This outside team can make or break a transaction! When your agent has a strong outside team to support you through the process means, you'll avoid so many headaches! Even if that outside resource is on the "buyer's side," your listing agent can ensure the deal goes through smoothly by recommending these good resources to the buyer and to the buyer's agent.

I've always believed that my great team of resources is one of my strongest assets because I've seen what can happen *without* such a team, literally hundreds of times: An inept escrow officer can completely screw up an escrow by miscalculating amounts due. An insurance agent can totally delay a close by not getting the right policy together in time. Another example: What if your buyer wants something fixed within a really short contingency period? Your listing agent can save the day by having just the right person to handle it on speed dial. You won't have to scramble around for a contractor who may or may not be good and may or may not get the job done in time.

Rapport

"Rapport" is a French word so, of course, it's hard to understand! Basically, it means that you feel "aligned" with someone. You not only get along with them, you feel that you're "kindred spirits." They "get" you. Maybe you have different backgrounds, even come from different cultures, but they "speak your language."

I know, this probably sounds like dating advice! But the point is that you'll be entrusting a precious possession, your home, to a total stranger. Not only is it the largest financial asset most of us have, but our homes often have a lot of emotional attachment as well. You want someone you really trust and who understands how important this sale is to you.

You probably have specific, important reasons and goals for selling your home (we'll talk about this in a later chapter) so you don't want some bulldozer of a listing agent to put *their* agenda before yours. You want someone who will not only guide you but who will *listen* to you. You'll be spending time and making important decisions with your listing agent. They don't have to become your very best friend, but you certainly don't want to get stuck with someone who irritates the heck out of you!

Savvy Seller Questions to Ask

I'll give you specific questions to ask about marketing and negotiation later. Here are some additional questions you can use to vet potential listing agents. I'd suggest you keep this list along with other questions you have right next to you during your first appointment, so you get the information you need to feel confident about your decision.

Credentials:

1. Are you a Realtor®? What resources from the NAR do you use?

2. What further courses have you taken in real estate? What did you learn from them?
3. (If they show you a certain credential) What does this credential mean? How will it help you sell my home?

Experience:

1. How much experience do you have selling homes like mine in this area? Can you give me some recent examples?
2. How many homes have you sold over your career? Is that you and your own team personally, or does it include other agents under your broker?
3. Do you specialize in my type of home? This geographic area? What makes this type of home and this area unique?
4. (If they have many years of experience) How would you say that real estate has changed over the last several years? Have you kept up with the latest trends in marketing to buyers online? What specifically do you do in that arena?
5. (If they have little experience) Do you have a more senior person who will be intimately involved in this listing? Who is that person?

Reputation: Though you can't really ask them directly what their reputation in the community is, you can ask:

1. Are you involved in the community and any professional organizations?

2. What do you like your clients and counterparts to say or think about you? What do you think you are known for as an agent?

Overall Team:

1. Who else is on your team? What are their skills and background?
2. What specifically do you handle versus what members of your team handle?
3. How often will I be interacting with them? With you?

To find a Savvy Seller Realtor near you, please visit www.IAmASavvySeller.com and we will connect you!

SAVVY MARKETING IN TODAY'S WORLD

The world has changed drastically over the last couple of decades, hasn't it? The way we shop, communicate, and get our news, information and entertainment has totally changed. Even in the last five years, things like online shopping and social media have exploded. With technology, we can pay bills and order our lattés with our smart phones. We can take a video of Junior taking his first steps and shoot it to Grandma thousands of miles away in seconds. We can find out where the nearest gas station is or how high Mt. Everest is (29, 029 feet!) with a two second Google search.

Yet despite our fantastic advances in technology, the real estate industry has lagged way behind. The vast majority of agents still do their jobs the same old way they did in the '80's, *especially* when it comes to marketing. Why do you care? Because basic traditional marketing will *not* get you the best result. They may be able to get your house sold but it will not happen as quickly as it could, and you won't get the price and most favorable terms you could get. Why? Because ***basic traditional marketing does not reach as many potential, qualified buyers***. Period.

So, though you don't need to be especially tech-savvy, your listing agent absolutely needs to be. And though you don't need to know how to take traditional marketing and put it on steroids, your listing agent needs to know how to do this. As a homeowner, you just need to know enough about these things so you can tell if the agents you're interviewing know what the heck they're talking about *before* you sign on the dotted line!

For example, many agents will tell you, "Yeah, sure, I market on social media." But what they're really saying is that they'll post something about your house on their business and personal Facebook pages. Who sees it? The people who already see those posts. That, my friends, is *not* how you market on social media!

Effective digital marketing targets all those folks who are *not* already connected. It captures potential buyers who *don't* visit that agent's website or Facebook pages. It's the difference between 12 people knowing that your home is on the market and 120,000 people knowing. In fact, my ads tend to get hundreds of hours of views. One recently got 555 hours compared to the average of 55 minutes others' ads get. (See page 70 to see graphics about Video Watch Time.) According to statistics in the NAR's Profile of a Home Buyer, *67% of buyers will walk through a home they see online*. So, imagine the difference between 55 min and 555 hours or 12 views and 120,000 views! It's like the dif-ference between singing in the shower versus singing at half-time during the Super Bowl. It's all singing but the real pros go for the Super Bowl gig!

Savvy Digital Marketing Power

I cannot stress enough how much the internet and social media can do to ensure the successful sale of your home, get you the most amount of money possible, expose it to the masses and get you the best terms! This type of marketing can get very technical, but you don't need to know all the technical ins and outs. All you need to know is how exactly your listing agent plans to tap this power for you. (See graphic example of Social Media Reach.) Good marketing *without* tapping the power of social media and the internet might attract dozens of prospective buyers. Good marketing on social media *can reach literally thousands*! And having more potential buyers exposed to your home *definitely* gives your home a competitive advantage.

Really effective marketing campaigns start *before* your home even goes on the market! Your agent should not only distribute "Pick your Neighbor" brochures and have a "Coming Soon" lawn sign prior to the official date (as long as allowable per NAR), they should also begin their social media and internet campaigns to get buzz going.

An exceptional agent will do **paid advertising** on social media which can get literally thousands of views. Your agent should also be creating cookies on the backend of their advertising to capture target audience. A savvy agent knows how to use paid *weekly* Facebook ad campaigns that are *targeted* to people "interested in moving" per Facebook analytics. They'll use services like Adwerx or Ylopo which analyze consumer behavior to target potential buyers looking in your area. They will do paid ads on social media sites with your property tour (this generates over 50,000+ views, hours of video watch time, and tons of comments, likes and shares!). They'll post on Craigslist to capture out of area leads. And they will post frequently on Instagram to reach the millennial market.

If your agent is really sharp, they won't just list your home on MLS, etc. They'll do weekly posts and updates of your home on various real estate sites to keep your home in top spots. They'll also do a "reverse prospecting search" to identify prospective buyers.

In everything they do, they will make sure that they have identified the potential buyers who are most likely to pay the highest price for your home. This becomes the *target market* they focus their efforts on. They don't just create boring ads and posts. They get creative with contests and giveaways that promote your home's virtual tour video. Also, in everything they post online, they'll research and use *search engine optimization (SEO)* to make sure the ads and posts about your home will get the most views. This means using titles, captions and content that features key words potential home buyers are using to find a home.

When it comes to online marketing and social media (which is my personal expertise and strength!), we often think of Facebook. But YouTube and Instagram are important also. In fact, YouTube is the world's second largest search engine after Goggle so videos of your home definitely should be there with great titles and captions. I also post all my listings in my blog so they get higher SEO (search engine optimization).

We also have a software that can track buyers' behaviors online and send them information about our properties that match up to the homes they are searching. We can then generate a list of those buyers and continue to market to them. It's pretty crazy what the technology can do.

Once they've placed ads and posts online, great agents don't just "set it and forget it." They have a *constant tracking system* that determines which ads are doing well and which need tweaking. They stay on top of the campaign and immediately contact any leads that come in from it personally *via phone or text.*

Tracking also allows an agent to be proactive and more effective. For example, if one of my homes has had a certain number of showings within a certain time period with no offers, I know it's time to reduce the price. This isn't my crystal ball talking. It's data. It's beyond just doing a market comparison analysis. My team analyzes the data of home sales and days on market for any given period, how much inventory is on the market, absorption rate, and whether it's a buyers' or a sellers' market. In some markets, fifteen showings in twenty-one days with no offer spells trouble. In a slower market or a hotter market, the criteria would be different. The point is that we take the time to analyze data and track our marketing results so we can continue to be proactive.

During the initial interview, you should ask to see examples of the agent's proposed listing and their social media analytics from past properties. I've given you an example of what my team uses in the back of this book on pages 70-74).

Traditional Marketing on Steroids

You're probably familiar with the basics of traditional marketing in real estate: The agent lists your property on MLS, makes up a flyer, sends out a mass email to other real estate agent, throws up their sign, puts some photos on their company website, and holds an open house or two. Done, right?

That is *not* how great agents today do it. They make sure that everything they do stands out and is unique and exceptional. And when they do that, your home stands out. These agents put their "traditional marketing" on steroids and the "traditional" part is only one step in the whole marketing strategy. Here's what those first traditional marketing pieces look like for the kind of exceptional listing agent you really want on your team:

MLS Listing: A great agent will not only list your home on MLS but on *all* of the real estate sites available like Zillow, Redfin, Realtor.com and Trulia. (There are actually hundreds of real estate sites and I market my listings on *all* of them.) A savvy agent will use the "back end" of these sites (when allowed or when they pay to do so) so they can make your listing more attractive and guarantee the property will stay in a primary position. They'll post a virtual video tour of your home rather than just a few photos. (Go to www.SellSavvyNow.com to see an example video tour.) In the listing, a great agent won't just post the basics with the same canned copy you see on every listing. They'll feature things that make your home unique and particularly attractive to potential qualified buyers—and they'll have done their research earlier to identify the most likely buyers and what they're looking for.

Professional Videos and Photos: Realtors™ who really care about doing a superior job for you won't just shoot a few photos and a quick video with their smartphone on the fly! They will *pay* to have a professional photographer and videographer come in to do the job. These pros will make sure to capture your home's best features, to ensure that unique aspects of your home stand out, that lighting is great, and that angles are inviting and give your home a sense of spaciousness. Then they'll take those photos and video and edit the heck out of them to give the biggest impact. They'll take pictures at night to capture your house if it looks great when it is all lit up. They'll do whatever it takes and spare no expense to show off your property to its best advantage.

Video is so critically important in marketing your home! Statistically, on social media like Instagram and Facebook, videos get *12 times more shares* than text or photos! So, when your home is posted using video, you get at least 12 times more people viewing it organically! And just imagine what happens when you put some *paid* ad spend behind the video (that's how we get thousands of views and hundreds of hours watched!). When a website has video on it, people spend 88% more time on that website. So, I take videos *very seriously* in marketing all of my listings.

In many cases, I'll use drones for parts of the video. The videos on all of my listings are 3D virtual reality tours that are interactive. It allows prospective buyers to feel like they're really there experiencing the home, even though they're sitting at home at their computers in their pajamas! Because it's so interactive, more viewers are engaged and stay watching it longer than they do with photos or regular videos alone. The technology I use is also linkable to all social media so it's like I'm hosting very cool open houses 24/7!

BTW, an incredibly awesome video that **doesn't get proper distribution** is like your grandmother's crystal wineglasses that are tucked away in some closet—beautiful but useless. 99% of agents will say they market using video, but they never take the time and energy to distribute it as it should be. My videos can get 555 hours of viewing time. Based upon how ineffectively most agents use social media and video, it's highly unlikely that they even get 5 hours of watch time!

Printed Materials: Rather than a cheap flyer, a great listing agent will spend the time and money to create a high-quality, full color brochure with links to the virtual video tour and website. They'll make sure this brochure gets sent to *everyone* who makes online or phone inquiries about your house or any similar homes in a digital copy, which is basically your home's website. And I make sure that all printed materials are cell phone compatible because **91% of buyers use cell phones** in their property search.

I also create a "Pick Your Neighbor" brochure and distribute it to *all* of your neighbors. Why? Because people who live in your same neighborhood tend to know people like themselves. Therefore, they're likely to know others who would like to live in your house and neighborhood. They've often got friends or even family members (the ones they like!) who are looking for new homes. We need to make sure everyone in the community knows that your home is available.

If your agent decides to do an open house (which actually isn't that effective in terms of selling homes in most cases), they'll give each visitor this high-quality brochure rather than just their business card. According to N.A.R. *less than 7%* of buyers found their home from an open house and a property sign. Open houses are ineffective but still used by many agents. Why? For one thing, it's a way they can prospect for new clients. It's also because they have been doing open houses for years and years, and they lack the skillset to reach potential buyers and market to them where they really look for new homes, which is online!

Engaging the Real Estate Community: A Realtor™ who has a good reputation definitely has a head start here! One with a rotten reputation, not so much. First, a great listing agent will create an attractive email with a link to the brochure, the website listing, and the virtual tour. Rather than just blasting this email out and hoping someone will open it, they'll target their emails to the best buyers' agents in the area, then they'll follow up with them personally. They'll make sure that buyers' agents in their own company keep the property top of mind.

I also send it to agents outside the area who have brought buyers into the community. Our team contacts preferred lenders for any prospective buyers in their pipeline. And when my clients' homes are being shown, my team will contact buyers' agents *within 24 hours after each showing* to get specific feedback to help guide our marketing campaign.

Lawn Signs: Most lawn signs are designed to promote the agent, not sell the home! A great agent will spend the money to create a distinctive sign that is lit at night. Why? Because more people will notice the sign at night while they're heading home and that's when many potential buyers drive through neighborhoods they're interested in. Rather than having a tacky plastic box with flimsy flyers (that almost always blow away in the wind!), today's best signs will have a customized texting feature that takes people directly to your home's website so they can view your home while sitting outside with the motor running. I also have technology in place that notifies my team when someone uses this feature so we can capture that potential buyer when they have just seen the house and its virtual tour. And we always call them right away. We know that when buyers are using this texting feature, they are very serious. (Or maybe it's just a nosey neighbor. But remember, they may know someone who is looking.)

Your Home's Website: Yes, your home should have its very own website, not just a crummy page with a few photos on the real estate company's website! Your home's website should be designed to be attractive with all the information a potential buyer needs: the virtual video tour, a photo gallery, the printable brochure, property map and information, mortgage calculator, and reports for out-of-town buyers showing an area map, area amenities, school scores and distance from the home, and community information. We love this feature and so do Buyers.

Does this sound like a lot of work? Honestly, it's just the tip of the iceberg in terms of what an *exceptional* listing agent can do for you. Yes, it requires *a commitment of time and money* to market your home. It requires a commitment on your agent's part to *continual education on technology and innovation*. This is what you *deserve* and what you should *expect* from your listing agent! And if it's not being done, then it is costing you money and time when it comes to selling your home.

Savvy Seller Questions to Ask

1. Specifically, what will you do to market this property?
2. What potential buyers would you target for my property and why? How specifically will you market to them?
3. What do you think makes my home most attractive to buyers and how will you feature it?

4. Can you show me examples of your brochures and other marketing materials? Are they cell-phone compatible?
5. Can you show me photos of your lawn signs? How will it stand out? Is there a text feature that captures buyers' information?
6. Do you use the back end of Zillow and other real estate sites? Are you a preferred agent on Zillow? (Zillow is the number one website buyers use to search properties.) On what sites will my home be listed? How often do you update these listings?
7. What kinds of efforts will you make to engage the real estate community about my property?
8. How will you engage my neighborhood?
9. What will my home's website look like? Who will take photos and videos?
10. What kind of social media ad campaigns will you run? How do you track them? How often will you post on various sites? How will you use their analytics?
11. Can you show me examples of reach, engagement, video views and time watched of your past home ads on social media? (If they gloss over this or can't answer, it tells you they aren't marketing correctly online which will cost you thousands of dollars.)
12. What kind of campaign do you run before the property officially goes on the market?
13. How do you specifically target buyers who are looking at properties similar to mine?

SAVVY NEGOTIATING FOR THE WIN

Negotiation has gotten a bad rap and is generally misunderstood. That's because many people think of negotiations like a big family-style dinner where there's not enough food to go around. Everyone has to beat out the other guy and get theirs before it's all gone! Others think of negotiating as just plain rude. If someone asks for something, you either give it to them or not. It's impolite to wheel and deal about it.

Both of these are totally outdated descriptions of what good negotiation should be. Good negotiation is based on the "win-win" concept. Everyone in the transaction gets what they *really* want and need, not necessarily absolutely everything they'd like. It's based on conscious compromise, give and take. And it's the most effective way to end up with the best price and most favorable terms for your home in the shortest amount of time!

Like marketing, you don't have to become an expert in negotiation yourself. But it's very important that you can identify what kind of negotiator the agents you're interviewing are and how much specific training they've had. To do that, let me give me a quick overview of negotiation styles:

The Competitive Negotiator

This is a "winner takes all" kind of negotiator. It's a very old school style of negotiation and, like the old "hard sell" from decades ago, it's not the most effective approach in today's world. An agent who is a competitive negotiator typically has a big ego and is proud to be known as cutthroat and unyielding. They might sell a lot of homes but it's usually at a high cost to their Seller (the deal takes much longer than it should, they end up with a high price but horrible terms, etc., etc.). You can recognize a competitive negotiator by the way they need to be right about *everything*! They are stubborn and inflexible, often not distinguishing between big issues and the unimportant ones. The competitive negotiator often relies on bullying techniques, like threatening to pull the deal or setting impossible timeframes for contingency periods or funding. This kind of approach does *not* speed up the process but usually ends up costing you money in the end!

This kind of agent might be charming to you as a client but tends to treat everyone else rudely and with disrespect. They can be short-tempered and unprofessional, even using profanity toward potential buyers and their agents. Their need to be superior and "right" ends up costing everyone unnecessary duress and money.

Why is an agent using this approach ineffective? Other agents don't like them, don't trust them, and know that they will be abusive during the transaction. So, they avoid bringing buyers to them. Or if they do, the buyer's agent approaches the transaction in full armor with rifles cocked! The stubbornness and inflexibility of a competitive negotiator will kill deals that could be viable or, when transactions do go through, leaves a bad taste in the mouths of everyone involved. It's simply not good business, and it won't get you the result you deserve.

We actually have a "blacklist" of agents who have done clients a disservice in the past, who have been totally unwilling to compromise even when it made sense for all parties, and who were just downright dirty. We present their offers, but we always warn our sellers of our past experiences if asked for an opinion.

The Compliant Negotiator

This kind of negotiator is the flip side of the competitive negotiator. Compliant people fear confrontation and disagreement. They need to be liked so they'll let others walk all over them. This type of agent will always give in to the demands of the other side—and will convince you to do the same. They might be a very nice person but not the person you need on your team.

Think of it like a surgical nurse who is afraid of blood. You wouldn't want that person assisting the surgeon who's operating on you! In the operating room, blood is just part of it. No one expects the patient to be wheeled in and, get completely healed without shedding a drop. A good nurse knows there's going to be blood. It's a necessary part of the process and it's not bad (unless it gets out of control!). While a fearful nurse closes their eyes at the sight of blood and avoids it altogether, a competent nurse takes it all in stride and manages the situation in the calmest way possible, knowing that it will lead to a healthy patient.

Like blood in the operating room, negotiation is just part of every real estate deal. It's something to be expected, not feared. It's extremely rare when a buyer steps up and accepts every single term that you as the Seller have proposed. It's not like customers in a department store who just look at the price tag and plunk down their credit cards. Real estate transactions are full of big issues and tiny issues, all of which require negotiation. If your agent simply caves every time the Buyer asks for something, they are *not* representing your best interests.

This type of agent always is warning you to cave in because "we may lose the deal." Don't fall for it. If a buyer wants your property badly enough, they'll negotiate. When my clients are nervous about losing a deal because we counter or negotiate, I always remind them that, if the buyer walks because our terms are not acceptable without countering back, they didn't want the house badly enough. They would have walked away anyway at some other time during the transaction and wasted our precious time.

Okay, so if it's not the bully and it's not the scaredy cat, what kind of negotiator do you want?

The Collaborative Negotiator

Like that calm surgical nurse, a collaborative negotiator expects and is prepared for negotiation. At its core, negotiation is communication. So, they'll listen and ask questions, seeking to really understand all parties to the transaction.

First of all, in collaboration with you, they've set goals for the sale of your home. They've helped you prioritize your needs and desires for the transaction. They may have even discussed areas of compromise with you prior to putting your home on the market. They won't promise you the moon but will help you be realistic from the get-go.

When offers come in, a collaborative negotiator will take the time to understand each Buyer's motivations and priorities by discussing them with the Buyer's agent. They'll do their research. When a conflict between what you want and what the Buyer wants arises, they'll work with the Buyer's agent to come up with creative options and solutions that work for everyone. They won't give away the farm and they'll always make sure that your most important priorities are honored. But they'll be willing to compromise on small issues that allow an otherwise great deal to go through. And if a dispute arises, they'll have the skills to keep the situation as calm as possible. They won't over-react to unreasonable demands or high emotions from the other side but will keep their cool and seek to understand the real issues beneath.

They won't let their ego or need for being right get in the way of getting the deal to go through as long as it is in the best interest of their Seller's goals and objectives.

To someone who is not trained specifically in negotiation, the collaborative approach might seem weak. But it's actually the strongest and most effective approach you can take. Just ask Harvard. The school has extensive trainings in this. It's the approach taught in virtually every advanced negotiation course these days. So, if your agent has taken some of these courses, that's a very good sign! Skills for collaborative negotiation include: effective verbal communication, great listening skills, rapport building, creative problem solving, assertiveness, and "ethical persuasion" skills. With these skills in their toolbelt, a collaborative agent will get you a much better end result than either of the other styles.

Your Job During Negotiations

You do have an important part to play in the negotiation. Your job isn't to deal directly with the Buyer or the Buyer's agent. In fact, no matter how great you are yourself as a negotiator, direct interaction on your part will only cause confusion and possibly derail the transaction. Let your agent do their job and support them. Your job is to:

Remember Your Priorities: In the next chapter, we'll talk about how to unearth your priorities for selling your home, which are those things that are most important to you.

During negotiations and within the contracts, you'll be making decisions on hundreds of issues. Some of them matter and some really don't. But it's easy to get caught up in all of it and lose sight of what you're really trying to accomplish by selling your home. Be sure and keep your priorities front and center so that when the inevitable kerfluffle happens, you won't lose your way.

Stay Calm and Think It Through: I know, I know, it's your *home* we're talking about! But the best decisions are *not* made when we're feeling emotional. Yes, you may be really ticked that the Buyer wants to charge you outrageous rent so you can stay a month after close. Yes, you may get freaked out when you hear they plan to fill in your swimming pool and remove the lemon trees you planted. Take a deep breath. *Respond, don't react.* Avoid a knee-jerk reaction and think it through. And if you need time to get into a better place emotionally, sleep on it before making a decision.

I remember in my earlier years in the business, I'd react and make decisions based upon emotions rather than facts. It's something that takes time and a lot of transactions to learn. Thank goodness, I've had over 2,000 transactions to get my emotions intact and to help my clients do the same.

Listen and Ask Questions: Your agent is there to advise so please listen. If you don't agree or understand why they want you to compromise on something, ask questions. Ask what their reasoning is. Ask about other options and, if you've thought of a different option, let them know. Ask them what will likely happen if you *don't* agree to the compromise. At the end of the day, you do have the final say in any decision. Just be sure to get all the information you need to make a good one.

Be Clear: Your listing agent wants to negotiate on your behalf so be as clear as you can. Keep communication open. If you don't like how the negotiation is going, tell them and explain why. When you make a decision or compromise, make sure it's one you feel good enough about that you will honor it. And if you're a couple selling your home, try to avoid mixed signals. Come to decisions together. Giving your agent clear marching orders allows them to represent you to the best of their ability. Then be willing to listen if your agent disagrees with the direction you want to take. They should be able to explain their alternative and why it is more beneficial to you.

Savvy Seller Questions to Ask

Unfortunately, most people don't find out what their agent's negotiating style is until they're in the middle of negotiations! Asking a few questions and really paying attention to how they interact with you will help.

1. What negotiations training and courses have you taken? What credentials do you hold in them? What did you learn from them?

2. How would you characterize yourself as a negotiator? What is your best skill in negotiating?
3. What do you think are the most important aspects of any negotiation?
4. What part will I play in negotiations and how will we communicate during this stage?

To find a Savvy Seller Realtor near you, please visit www.IAmASavvySeller.com and we will connect you!

SAVVY COMMUNICATION IS KEY

Another major area you want to screen for in a potential listing agent is *communication*. Too many traditional listing agents get you to sign on the dotted line then disappear for a month or so until they have an offer in hand—or to tell you why they *don't* have an offer. In this age of instant communication, that is simply not acceptable! You deserve more and should expect more, and you don't want to end up having to chase your agent down to get your important questions answered.

You want to know what's going on with the marketing. You want to hear about any comments made by potential buyers looking at your home. You want to give your input into the process and make sure your interests are really being served. Make sure you receive the kind of communication you need from the beginning.

For example, even during the initial listing appointment, a really great agent will take the time to explain what's happening in your market and how that will affect the sale of your home and its pricing. They'll tell you who your most likely buyers will be and how they intend to market to them. They'll give you honest feedback on your expectations for the sale and maybe offer alternatives to expectations that aren't realistic. They won't just schmooze you and talk over your head.

In fact, if three out of the four agents you interview say your home is overpriced, don't believe that fourth guy who says, "Hey, no problem!" He'll only waste your time when three months down the road he suggests reducing it! I can't tell you how many times I've seen a listing go to an agent who overstates the listing price when I was frank and honest about it. Then I'll see the home sit on the market for months and watch price drop after price drop until it finally sells for *less* than I could have gotten for it! The agent you want will treat you with respect as a valued partner in the process and not lead you on like this.

An example: A couple in our community had listed their home with an agent who said he could sell it for $749,000. Three weeks later, they reduced the price to $699,000. After 39 days on the market and very few showings, the couple took their home off the market. Thirty days later, they listed with my team. We were able to sell the home in just 9 days at $695,000—exactly the listing price they *should* have had from the beginning!

So, make sure your agent is frank, honest, and open with you. And this good communication should continue after you sign a listing agreement with them.

Savvy Communication is Key

Starting Off on the Right Foot

From the very beginning, your listing agent and their team should be in almost constant contact. Not in a way that harasses you or makes them inefficient, but in a way that keeps you informed about what is happening and when it's happening.

The first thing they should ask you is how to best connect with you. Do you prefer phone? Text? Email? What times of day are good? Your agent should also be clear about when they are available and who to contact for pressing questions if they aren't. I give all my clients contact numbers for all of the players on my team they'll be interacting with.

Here are just some of the things your agent and their team should be asking and communicating to you at the start:

Your goals and needs from this sale. I cover this more thoroughly in in the next section. But your listing agent should take the time to sit down with you and really understand what you want and need from this sale. They should be sincerely interested and pay careful attention to what you have to say. A good agent will listen and ask questions so they can tailor their marketing and negotiation strategies accordingly. If they gloss this part over and don't get into depth with you on this, that's definitely a red flag! It very well might mean that they'll be using "off the shelf" strategies they've always used—and you'll get an "off the shelf" result in the end.

Your home's best features. Who knows this better than you? Your agent should ask for your input about what you most like about the home and what makes it great to live in. A great listing agent (or their marketing specialist) should ask you about the features of your home and any upgrades you've done. They should ask about the specific location including great neighbors, terrific neighborhood hot spots, and public amenities nearby. Of course, they'll have a lot of area statistics and knowledge at their fingertips. But your personal insight into these things, whether it's neighborhood schools or local hair salons, will add a lot to the marketing of your home.

Your home's information. Okay, this is the boring part but it's necessary. I call it my "Seller's Homework" and I've created a special packet for my clients that takes them through all we need. It asks for things like alarm codes and desired showing instructions (i.e. "please give owner at least 30 minutes notice" or "do not allow pets outside"). It also includes forms to help my clients provide all the information they need to provide legally to prospective buyers.

In California and many other states, the amount of information you have to disclose is incredible! Your agent should not only talk you through what's required but also provide forms and processes that make it less burdensome! For example, I provide my homeowners with a complete checklist that covers everything from homeowners' associations to how old the roof is. For the required disclosures, I provide them with an easy online form. I tell my clients to pour themselves a glass of wine, open up their laptop or tablet, then walk from room to room and make notes of any repairs or changes they've made over the years. When it comes to filling out State-required disclosures, we go into detail with our clients explaining what each line item means. (Sadly, many listing agents simply hand their clients these complicated forms and ask them to fill them out. This is not only a hassle for you but can cause legal problems down the line if you don't do it correctly and completely.)

My state, California, is very strict about disclosures and you have to disclose *anything* that has ever been modified, repaired, replaced, added, fixed or changed. You have to disclose *anything* you know about that "may" happen in the future or that did happen in the past to the home, city, neighborhood, etc. It's not up to you to decide if it's good or bad, significant or not, even if something is obvious or not. You still need to disclose it. So, if you live on a golf course, disclose it no matter how obvious that seems. If you don't and a golf ball hits the house and damages someone or something, you may be open to a lawsuit. I am *not* kidding!

Those "boiler plate" disclosures in your forms cover a lot, but over-disclosure is always better if you want to avoid future lawsuits. (I've taken classes showing me how to fill out the disclosures properly to keep my clients safe from litigation.) If you have a lot of traffic or live on a busy street, disclose it. If you changed out the toilet seat in 2005, disclose it. If you know about any future change to the community, disclose. If you have an HOA and you know dues are going up, disclose it. Yes, it's a pain to note all these things, but it's much less stressful than a lawsuit!

Setting up initial appointments. Your agent's team should not only let you know when things are happening but should schedule times that are convenient for you, not just for them. You'll have an appointment for photos and videos to be taken and they should also send you a checklist of how to prepare for this appointment. I always arrange to have a stager come to my clients' home to make suggestions about how to best show off its features and do some basic staging with them.

Your agent's team will schedule installation of a lawn sign and should ask for your input before placing it. They'll also have a lock box installed and someone should sit down and explain to you exactly how this will work, who will have access to your home and when they'll have access. I also always give my clients tips on how to keep valuables safe during the period when a home is being shown.

Home Preparation: Before your home goes on the market, a good listing agent should provide you with a checklist of repairs and any improvements they recommend. And your agent should take the time to discuss this list with you explaining why certain things are important then help you come up with alternatives, if necessary. I also give my clients a list of our preferred vendors (who have been screened and vetted) for any work that needs doing or to get estimates. (I'll talk more about how to get your home market ready in the next chapter.)

Communication During the Marketing Stage

Sadly, this is the stage when too many listing agents go silent! They might be working on your behalf, but they don't bother to keep you in the loop. But a really good listing agent will involve you. First of all, they'll lay out exactly what they intend to do to market your property *before* they even get started. They'll tell you where and when certain pieces will be coming out. They'll make sure you get copies of all printed and electronic marketing pieces so you can share them. They'll tell you the best way to share on your social media and create emails you can forward to friends and family.

When the marketing phase begins, you should get updates on progress at least weekly! Personally, my team sends out a marketing report twice per week. The report details the ads and posts we put out that week and give a detailed analysis of the results (how many leads, how many showings, etc.) We also send updates on any market changes like mortgage interest rate fluctuations, absorption rate, and sales trends that might affect the salability or marketability of your home.

Your listing agent should also be getting and sharing feedback from buyers' agents after they've shown the property. Waiting three months to find out that buyers all think your carpet needs replacing is a waste of time! We install synched lock boxes that tell us in real time when a home is shown. Then someone on our team calls buyer's agent within twenty-four hours of each showing and asks for feedback. We share that feedback with our clients in our twice-weekly reports and discuss whether any changes need to be made.

Most importantly, your listing agent should be tracking and analyzing the results from different marketing efforts. And they should respond quickly to whatever trends they see! For example, if an ad on social media isn't generating any leads, it needs to be tweaked. If the home is being shown frequently but is getting no offers, maybe the price or something in the home itself needs to be tweaked. If the brochure doesn't generate any phone calls from potential buyers, it needs to be tweaked. A great agent will stay on top of this and make sure you're kept informed.

During Negotiation

This is the period when you and your agent should have the most one-on-one time. People on your agent's team may handle many different parts of a transaction, but when it comes to negotiation, your listing agent should be totally hands-on and never leave negotiation to a junior person who has no experience or training! In my case, I have several agents on my staff who have earned advanced certifications in negotiation. I oversee the process but I'm confident in them.

First of all, your agent should share any information they have about the buyer regarding their hot buttons, needs, and motivations. They should also be able to share with you what they know about the buyer's agent: what type of negotiator they are, how communicative and reliable they are, other transactions they've closed, etc.

As offers come in, your agent should be able to give you good, clear feedback on how viable the offers are and show you data to back up their conclusions. They will also point out where each offer might be countered to get closer to what you want. This should not be a "my way or the highway" kind of discussion but a collaborative give and take with your agent. I'm very aware that I know more about real estate and this market than any of my clients and that it's my job to come up with creative counters and solutions to differences between their goals and the offers that come in. That said, I respect my clients as intelligent people and always ask for their input during this entire phase.

During Escrow

Honestly, for most Sellers, this is the most frustrating stage! It's a waiting game to see if all the contingencies clear. It's a waiting game while the title company does its report. It's a waiting game to see when the lender will finally release funding and the title can be recorded. And let me just tell you that during this stage, lots of "stuff" happens.

Personally, I don't believe that my clients need to know about every tiny hiccup in this phase. But I do think they should be informed immediately of anything that might derail the transaction. Some agents believe they should "wait and see" if the worst eventually will happen. Honestly, I think they're just afraid to face giving their clients bad news! Your listing agent should respect you enough to let you know if problems arise that may squelch the deal or cause it to change dramatically.

My first broker taught me that it's our jobs as agents to be problem solvers and that problems will *always* come up somewhere during a transaction. So many different people have parts to play in getting to a successful conclusion. I believe that it's *my* job to know *their* jobs and to stay on top of what's happening, rather than sitting back and assuming everything is just peachy keen. A good agent will constantly check in with the various participants and verify that the process is on track.

For example, if your agent finds out that the roof inspection came back with issues you didn't know about, you want to know sooner rather than later so you can decide what to do. If it looks like the buyer might not be able to qualify, your agent should tell you and get some back-up offers going. Hopefully, they asked the right questions prior to going into escrow to keep this from happening in the first place. But sometimes, things just come up. Someone missed something or forgot to ask the proper questions or didn't verify the proper information. You don't want to get to the very end of the loan contingency period to discover that the lender never intended to fund the loan!

What about working with the title company? Too many agents simply turn you over to the escrow officer and call it good. The great agents I know don't. Like me, they'll stay on top of the escrow and make sure all the players are getting documentation in on time, that it's correct, and it goes as smoothly as possible.

Savvy Seller Questions to Ask

You don't want to find out that you've hired a poor communicator six months down the line when you're trying to chase your agent down to find out what the heck is going on! Here are a few questions you might ask to see if the agents you're interviewing will really keep you informed and involved:

1. How often will your team communicate with me? Who on your team is my main contact person during each phase?
2. How can I reach you if I have an urgent question? Who do I call if I can't reach you?
3. What types of checklists or consultation do you give to help me get my home ready for market?
4. How often will I hear about your marketing efforts and the results we're getting? How much detail will you provide?
5. How often will you give me feedback about what potential buyers and their agents are saying about the property?
6. How will we stay in touch during negotiations?
7. How hands-on is your team during the contingency period? How do they coordinate with the escrow and the title company? How often will you give me updates?

CREATE SAVVY SELLER GOALS AND PRIORITIES

When people decide to sell their home, they don't just wake up one morning and say, "Let's put the house on the market!" They've usually thought about it for a while and often have more than one motivation behind the sale. And for couples selling, they often have different, even conflicting motivations. (BTW, this is true of buyers too. They'll start a home search—often online—3-6 months prior to being ready to pull the trigger. This is why it's important that your agent knows how to capture potential buyers who were searching previously.)

To get the best result, the result that makes you happiest at the end of the day, it's *critically* important that you sit down and get very clear on *why* you're selling your home and *your particular goals* in selling your home. Without this information, even the best Realtor® will have trouble delivering for you.

Create Savvy Seller Goals and Priorities

Why? **Because your agent's strategy is** (or *should* be) **based on your individual goals and needs**. This includes their strategy for both marketing and negotiation. Yes, they may do the same basics for all of their listings. But they should also be tailoring these strategies to your needs and priorities.

Let's take someone who needs to move quickly to take care of a sick parent across the country. They don't want to leave too much money on the table, but they're more concerned about getting out of town ASAP with enough to pay off their mortgage. Contrast that scenario with a couple who isn't in a hurry, who wants to sell so they can upgrade, and who wants to get the most money they can out of the house.

Even if these homes were exactly the same in the exact same neighborhood, a good listing agent would approach them differently. They might recommend the second seller does some minor renovation or landscaping while they might recommend that the first seller clears out immediately so the house can be immediately occupied. With the second seller, they might push the price a bit (without going crazy) to see how the market responds. For the first seller, they might suggest a price that is just slightly below market.

In my experience, in any transaction, there are a million aspects that can be tweaked depending on my client's goal and needs. Things like length of escrow, cash versus obtaining a loan, renovations or none, contingencies or as-is, rent back or none, high or low deposit, back up offer or not, etc., etc. However, if you aren't very clear on what you need and want from the sale of your house, your agent simply can't develop the best strategy.

And during the sale process, you'll have dozens of decisions to make! If you take the time to get clear up front, making those decisions will be much easier and less stressful while your house is on the market and during negotiations.

Get Clarity

Sit down and write down all the things that are important to you in the sale of your house. Be sure and write down *everything* that comes to you. And as you write these things down, ask yourself, "Why?" For example, maybe you write, "Sell the house for $650,000." Why do you want to sell it for $650,000? Is it because your neighbor sold his house for that much? Is it because that's how much you need to pay off your mortgage and have enough for the down payment on your next home? Is it because you're trying to fund your retirement? Get very specific about the reasons *why* what you want or need is important to you. (And by the way, how much you *net* out of the sale is more important to you than the selling price, right?) Just because you want or need a certain amount out of your house doesn't mean it is worth that much. Bottom line, your home is only worth what a buyer is willing to pay in any given market.

Think about what you *don't* want as well. Maybe you don't want your house to be shown at certain times. Maybe you don't want to repair certain things that you know should be repaired. Maybe you don't want to clear out your overstuffed garage before your house goes on the market. List all of those things you *don't* want and think about *why* you don't want them. Keep in mind that any restrictions you place on the sale will lessen the number of buyers and offers you attract. Talk to your Realtor™ and ask about the impact of your restrictions then make a decision from there.

Clarity for Couples

When I have my Sellers do this process and they are selling as a couple, I often recommend that each person comes up with their own separate list. Why? Sometimes, one partner is hesitant to contradict the other or to be totally frank about what they want. Doing it separately gives each one a little more freedom.

After you each have made up your own individual lists, sit down together and compare them. Talk each item through. Notice which goals and desires you share. You might surprise each other with new ideas or possibilities. You may find areas where the two of you are rowing in different directions! If you have conflicts, it's important that you find this out now. It will save you many headaches down the road if you can resolve your differences now. After you've brought your agent on board, you want to present a united front so they can be clear about what you want and don't want from the sale and during the sales process.

Get Your Priorities Straight

In life, we rarely get *absolutely everything* we want! Selling your home is no different. You may luck out and have everything fall into place perfectly. But just in case they don't, you want to be clear on where you're willing to compromise and where you aren't.

For example, on your goals you may have written down that you don't want to do any renovations whatsoever to your home. Two weeks in, your agent is getting feedback from buyers' agents that the shiny black walls in your entry, living and dining rooms are very off-putting. If you're determined to get your price in a reasonable amount of time, you may need to suck it up and repaint.

I give my clients an analysis as to what they should fix up or not and how that will or will not affect their bottom line. For example, if it only costs $4,000 to paint the entire house but you can get $20,000 more if you do, it's worth considering. If you and your agent think some work would be worth it and can get you this kind of return but you don't have the cash, ask if it can be taken out of escrow or if the agent has options where they can pay to have it fixed up, then get reimbursed from escrow. Our office offers this service, and it's helped clients receive thousands and thousands more by doing the necessary repairs.

Here's an example of the value of minor repairs: A couple had listed their home with an agent who didn't mention anything about repairs or improvements. The house sat on the market at $629, 950 then was reduced to $599,950. After three months and no sale, the owners took it off the

Create Savvy Seller Goals and Priorities

market. Two months later, they listed with my team. We immediately recommended that they do a few repairs and upgrades at a cost of $3,300. We then professionally staged the house and listed it at its original $629, 900. Within ten days, we had an offer at $634, 000 (which successfully closed very quickly). In other words, they made $34,000 more than their "reduced price" by investing just $3,300! This is the kind of advice a good agent will give you. Because that former agent didn't give them this advice, not only did the home not sell, but they had to incur the expense of the mortgage, taxes, and utilities during that time. If they'd had this advice upfront, they could have made and saved $47,000 over that "reduced price!"

Back to your goals: Next, take your list and start prioritizing. If you could only have one of your goals, what would it be? If you could have three, which would they be? Keep going until you've got the whole list in "most important" to "least important" order.

Once you've completed and prioritized your list, share it with your listing agent. (I even ask people for their list at our first appointment.) They'll be able to give you feedback, make suggestions, and strategize to get you as much of that list as possible. The agent you really want to work with will be honest enough to tell you if some of what you want is unrealistic. They'll explain why and help you come up with a more reasonable expectation.

This is also the time to check "emotion versus fact." For sentimental reasons, you may really want to keep your daughter's room (the one who's away at college and about to get married) intact just as she left it. But if her Goth décor is scaring buyers off, you might need to reconsider and pack her stuff up.

Or maybe you're determined to get as much for your home as your snooty neighbor did last year. Is that based on fact or pride? "Fact" would mean that the market is the same or better as it was when the other house sold, that your home is located as favorably on the exact same or larger lot size, and that your house is exactly the same as his with all the same upgrades. "Pride" would be, "Because my house is just as good!"

I can't tell you how many times I've met with Sellers who want to receive the *highest* amount of money for their home. They think their home is worth more than everyone else's. However, when they go to buy, they want the biggest house with the most upgrades for the *least* amount of money. And, hey, I get where they're coming from. I'm the exact same way when I go to sell my own home and buy a new one! That's emotional attachment, not reality.

Listing price is often subject to "emotion over fact." If you've taken great care of your home and spent lots of money on awesome upgrades, you might be able to command a higher price—and you might not. Things like a swimming pool are very expensive but often don't get good return on the dollars you spent for it. The next owner may actually want to tear out that custom mantel you loved and spent a small fortune on. Listing price isn't justified solely by the amount of time and money you've put into your house. It's determined by the market. This is where you need to trust your agent. And if you've taken the time to choose a really good agent, you *can* trust their advice. (Just keep in mind that getting a real estate license and printing a business card doesn't necessarily make someone an advisor who should be trusted.) Listen when they tell you what your optimal listing price should be based on your goals and the market. Ask them to explain and show you the research that supports their suggested price and marketing strategy.

Once your home hits the market and especially during negotiations, keep your prioritized list handy to help you make those big and small decisions. Use it as a guide to remind you of what's important and what isn't. This guide will make the process a heck of a lot easier for both you and your agent. It will take the pressure off any decisions because you won't be "re-thinking" yourself at every turn. And at the end of the day, you are way more likely to achieve those important goals you've set!

Here are some questions to help you get started with your wants and needs list but don't stop with these. Try to be as broad and as clear as you can.

Savvy Seller Questions to Ask

1. Why are we selling our home?
2. Why at this particular time? Is this a "want to sell" or a "need to sell" time?
3. How quickly do we want to sell? How quickly do we really need to sell?
4. When do we want to move? Are we willing to vacate the home before it goes on the market? Do we want to rent back from the new owner if it closes before a certain date?

5. How much money do we want to net out of the sale? Why?
6. How soon do we need the funds?
7. How much money and effort are we willing to put into the house *before* it hits the market? What about changes or repairs requested by Buyer? Why will we do or not do these things?
8. Are we looking to repurchase? Locally or out of the area? Do we need help with that? (Your listing agent may be able to find you a good Buyers agent to work with.)

To find a Savvy Seller Realtor near you, please visit www.IAmASavvySeller.com and we will connect you!

SAVVY SELLER'S PREP FOR A GREAT SALE

I've mentioned a few ways you can help in terms of marketing and clarity about your goals and decisions. But making sure your home is market-ready is another huge way you can contribute to the successful sale of your home! Before even considering any renovations, most homeowners have plenty they can do to make their homes more attractive and make them more likely to breeze through inspections.

Set Up Your Home to Inspire Offers

Basically, you want your home to not only look clean and attractive, you also want *prospective Buyers to be able to see themselves and their families living there*. You want them to walk around and visualize where their piano could go and where their winter clothes could be stored. You want them to imagine themselves sitting in your tub or cooking dinner for friends in your kitchen. So, though the way you have your home set up right now might be perfect for you, it's important to look at it from the perspective of others who might want to live there. Make this a project for your whole family and get everyone on board and doing their part.

Some things to consider:

Your Closets: Many of us jam as much as we can into our closets! We might have shoes piled on the closet floor or our collection of golf hats crowding the shelves above. Though your closet may be spacious, if it's crowded, it will look as if it isn't. And if it's *not* spacious, that fact will become painfully obvious. It's worth the time to do some Spring cleaning. This might be a good time to get rid of clothes you no longer wear. If not, then box up as much as you can and hide it under the bed if need be. This goes for the closets in all bedrooms, your coat closet, your kitchen pantry and cupboards—every place you store things. Yes, potential buyers will not only be checking out closets but also kitchen cupboards, linen closets, and even bathroom medicine cabinets! It's not just that people are nosey (though some definitely are!) but they are trying to imagine fitting their stuff into where your stuff is. I always tell my clients, "Hey, you have to pack up anyway, so why not start now?"

Your Clutter: Few of us live in totally uncluttered homes, especially if we're active and have an active family.

Personally, I have a stack of books on the nightstand next to my bed that might kill someone in a bad earthquake! When my kids were younger, they picked up their toys, but they had scads of them in every room in the house. I have a home office that has all kinds of paperwork, resource materials, and electronics in it. A friend of mine who sews has a sewing machine, a serger, a dress form, hundreds of patterns and shelves full of material that are all squeezed into the guest bedroom.

Your mission here is to minimize the clutter! Box up stuff you don't access frequently. Keep stuff that you use often in an accessible place but hidden away. If your house is messy, Buyers get the impression that your home may not have been well-maintained. They'll get wary and look at everything about the home with a suspicious eye. So, though it might seem like a hassle, keep the goal in mind—and remember that it's not forever.

Your Housekeeping: Most of my clients hate this part. Most of us keep our homes relatively clean but the standard here is sparkling, market-ready clean. I usually suggest that my clients start with a great Spring cleaning that includes things like windows, fireplaces, overhead fans, baseboards, and vents. Get any tile grout spiffed up. Shampoo carpets and rugs. Polish floors. Wipe down doggy doors. Touch up paint and patch holes in the walls.

Once the major clean is done and your home starts to be shown, keep that standard up as much as possible. You never know when that perfect Buyer will ask to see your home! Kitchens and bathrooms should be especially clean with sparkling floors. You may need to sweep, mop, and vacuum more often because of all the people trooping through your house.

Your Furniture: Don't panic! I'm not going to suggest that you buy all new furniture! Just take a look and consider if your furniture really shows off your home's assets. Your agent or someone on their team should be able to help with this. Oftentimes, it's a question of simply rearranging furniture to make a room look more spacious and welcoming. Other times, you may want to consider removing pieces of furniture (like extra dining room chairs or that super-huge sofa) and storing them to open a room up. Moving a lamp can give a room better light. Adding pillows to a sofa can hide its worn spots. In some situations, a house actually shows better if the owner moves out and it's totally empty! If this is an option for you, discuss it with your agent.

Your Personal Stuff: By "personal stuff," I mean things like family photos, posters of rock bands or political slogans, the deer heads from your hunting adventures, those funny magnets and your kids' art that you have on your refrigerator. Again, the objective is for potential buyers to see *themselves* in this home, not you. Think about it: When you walk into someone's personal home for the first time, it can be a little awkward. You feel like an outsider and that you "don't belong," right? When you walk into a model home, you feel freer, not like an intruder. By hiding away a lot of what says "you" about the house, buyers are able to see more of "me" in it. I always advise my clients to make their homes as model-like as possible by removing most of their personal stuff.

Your Home's Nose: In California where I live, wine is big business and every wine drinker will tell you that wine has "a nose." You experience a wine's smell before you even take a sip. And consciously or unconsciously, potential buyers "smell" your home before they even look around! You may not even notice the smell of your home because you're used to it. But others will notice, and the scent can set the tone of the showing. (Who knew, right?!?) If your home smells musty or like your pets or has unpleasant cooking odors, it will turn people off. If it smells like cigarette smoke, some people will refuse to enter the house! If the odors are major, you may need to bring in professionals to clean and deodorize (or replace) carpets and furniture or even paint walls. If it's minor, you can often resolve it by using a scented plug-in and opening some windows, if it's nice weather.

Curb Appeal: Curb appeal is like that first impression you have of people. Once you have that impression, especially if it's not a good one, it's hard to change it! You don't have to spend a ton of money on this, but simple things like a freshly painted mailbox or new hardware on the front door can make a big difference. Make sure the lawn is mowed and any hedges or shrubs are trimmed. I usually suggest planting some colorful seasonal flowers in flower beds in the front yard and placing a few flowerpots on the front step. Wash down the front driveway and porch then roll up your hose and hide it. New welcome mats not only add eye appeal but will help remind potential buyers to wipe their feet!

Breeze Through Inspections

There are certain maintenance items regarding your home that you should take care of prior to putting your home on the market. Why? When a home inspection person can tick off certain items as being good and orderly, it tells the buyer that your home has been well maintained. Also, in some jurisdictions, the lender will not let a sale go through until certain items are in good repair and working properly.

Basic Maintenance: here is the checklist I give my clients with questions about the home repair items they should handle before we put the home on the market:

Is your water heater double strapped?
Do all of your smoke detectors work?
Do you have a CO 2 detector on each floor?
Have your furnace filters been changed recently?
Has your HVAC unit been professionally maintained recently?
Does your garage door open smoothly and does your garage door opener operate properly?
Do any of your doors or sliders need some WD40?
Do you have any leaky faucets or slow-flowing drains?
Do you have any missing or torn screens?
Do you have any light bulbs that need replacing?

Do all of your blinds and shades work properly?
Do all door locks and locking mechanisms work properly?
Are your gates and their latches working properly? Is your fence in good repair?

Major Repairs

What about things like mold and dry rot issues, leaks, broken roof tiles, health and safety issues or termite problems? If you know that these problems exist, I almost always recommend that you take care of them *before* your home goes on the market. Often, lenders will *not* fund a home until these problems are fixed. Even if they did, few home buyers want to take on that kind of project. Delaying getting this work done will only delay the sale and may actually turn some buyers away. If you absolutely cannot afford to have this work done, *at the very least* get a guaranteed estimate from a reputable vendor so your potential buyers have a sense of what they would be getting into.

What about other major issues like a roof that is leaking? First of all, it's illegal to withhold that information if you know or even suspect your home has a problem. Even if you could withhold it, any intelligent buyer will have a thorough home inspection done during the contingency period. In the worst case, your buyer may cancel the contract as soon as they find out about the roof. In the best case, they will probably ask to have the sales price discounted substantially. Why? Because when you have problems with major systems, such as roofs, structural, plumbing, electrical or mechanical systems, you really don't know what you're getting into until you get into it! A vendor may say they can repair rather than replace something but unless the problem is very straightforward, they can't be sure.

In a perfect world, I'd have you do what it takes to make that roof sound (with a guarantee). If that's not a possibility, just be aware that it causes an obstacle to the sale that will have to be overcome.

What about major renovations, like updating bathrooms or kitchens? This is such a case by case decision that I won't even get into it here. It's a discussion you need to have with your agent. When I discuss this possibility with my clients, I make sure to give them all the data they need to make a good decision. We'll talk about trends in the market and the likely return on their investment for these renovations. We'll get estimates from my preferred vendors. We'll talk about the time involved and how far back that will push putting the house on the market. We'll talk about any disruption the family might go through while the renovations are happening. It's important to weigh all of these factors before making this decision.

ON THE MARKET: SAVVY SELLER DO'S AND DON'TS

Woo hoo! Your house is ready, your listing agent has started their dynamic marketing campaign, and your home is officially on the market! Good for you! Now I'd like to help you succeed during these next stages. Over my years of experience and after literally thousands of home sales, I've come up with a list of simple do's and don'ts for my clients. Unfortunately, I've arrived at some of these do's and don'ts based on clients' innocent missteps—that led to horrendous results! So, I don't take them lightly!

Showing Your Home

When you get that call that an agent wants to show your home, here's how you help your house shine (and if you're away at work during the day, do these things before you leave in the morning):

Keep all lights on. Visitors shouldn't have to fumble for light switches, and it makes your home appear brighter, more inviting, and easier to see.

Place Glade Hawaiian Breeze scented plug-ins throughout the home. This gives a nice but not overwhelming scent.

Keep all blinds and window treatments open. This will make your home seem larger and brighter. If you can, remove window screens to let as much light as possible in and give an open feel. (Save them in the garage because the buyer will want them later.) It will also show off your exterior features.

Put away any clutter and personal stuff. In your preparation, you already did this so all you should have to do is put away anything that was brought out the day before.

Spiff up your kitchen and bathroom. The whole house should be clean but make sure to do a last polish of these two areas. Flush toilets. Fold towels and washcloths. Wipe down counters and sinks. Empty trash cans.

Sweep your front step and front hall. It's about first impressions. It's also about not having debris for agents and buyers to track into the home that you're working so hard to keep clean!

Make arrangements for pets (if any) during showings. Personally, I love animals but not everyone does. A really terrific buyer might just be terrified of good old Fido. Figure out what you can do with your furry loved ones. You could take them to a neighbors', keep them in a space in the yard or garage, take them with you, or even drop them off at kitty or doggy day care?

Be absent during the showing. You want potential buyers to feel free to really explore your home and "occupy" it. You want them to speak frankly to their agent about what they like and don't like about the house. You want them to turn on the disposal, poke into the garage, pace off your dining room. Even if you sit quietly at your desk minding your own business, your very presence will make the situation awkward.

Now for a very important **Don't**:

Don't say a thing. I've trained my clients and they're really good about being somewhere else during a showing. But sometimes, they get home and the buyer and their agent are still there. If that happens, be pleasant, make yourself scarce, and do NOT engage in conversation! Why? By answering even seemingly harmless questions, you can sabotage your position in the whole negotiation process! Does this sound paranoid? Let me give you an example: A client of mine came home to find the buyer and their agent still there. She started chatting innocently with agent who asked, "So, why are you moving?" My seller explained that her mother was terminally ill and that she was moving to take care of her. The agent then made a few comments about how the market was slow (it wasn't), few people were offering cash (lots were), and his client was rare in wanting this kind of home (he wasn't). With that leverage, the agent came in with a low-ball offer and a very fast close. Even though we had just started our marketing, my client panicked and almost took the offer. I was able to talk her off the ledge and we ended up getting a substantially higher offer that closed quickly and without hassle.

There's an old slogan from World War II: "Loose lips sink ships." Don't sink your ship.

A LAST WORD

Honestly, there's so much more I could tell you about selling your home! But armed with the information from this book, you now know more than 99% of all homeowners. I hope you've learned a lot and gotten some ideas and inspiration. I also hope that you are hugely successful in selling your home!

If I can answer any questions or offer assistance, please feel free to contact me a 925-325-HOME (4663). And be sure to go to www.SellSavvyNow.com for informational videos that are easy to watch and full of valuable information. We can also get you a Free Marketing Analysis and a Home Evaluation of your home.

Wishing you the best!

Krista Mashore

To find a Savvy Seller Realtor near you, please visit www.IAmASavvySeller.com and we will connect you!

SOCIAL MEDIA ANALYTICS FOR PAST PROPERTIES

Circled in bold are the hours people have watched these property tour videos. 555 hours of watch time, 394 hours of watch time, 208 hours of watch time, and 357 hours of watch time on these particular videos!

Social Media Analytics for Past Properties

Homes By Krista
Published by Krista Vitale Mashore [?] · July 1 at 5:31pm ·

Absolutely Stunning Home For Sale in Brentwood!
$1,099,000
6 Bedrooms + Loft & Movie Room
4 Bathrooms
3 Car Garage
4,680 Sq. Ft
16,551 Sq. Ft Lot
Built in 2011
Gourmet Kitchen
Custom Crown & Wainscoting
Plantation Shutters Throughout
Outdoor Cabana w/ Full Kitchen
Gorgeous Inground Pool w/ Waterfalls & Fire Features

Text "3256572" to 79564 for Additional Information & Details

132,974 people reached

79K Views

👍 Like 💬 Comment ↗ Share   ⟳ View Results

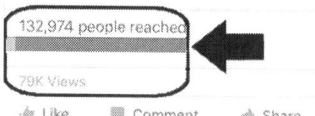 These results are AMAZING!   Top Comments ▾

97 shares

132,974 people reached means that many people saw this ad for this home! 468 people reacted to this post, which means, they like, loved, were shocked, etc. by this post. Also, 97 people shared this post!

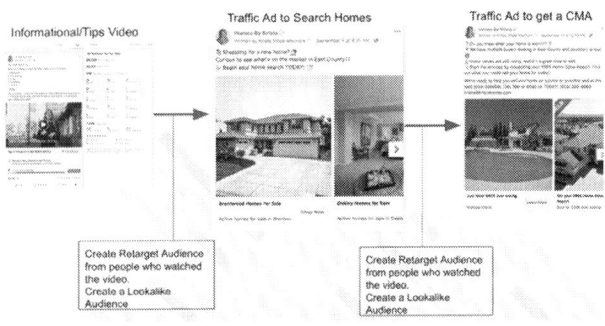

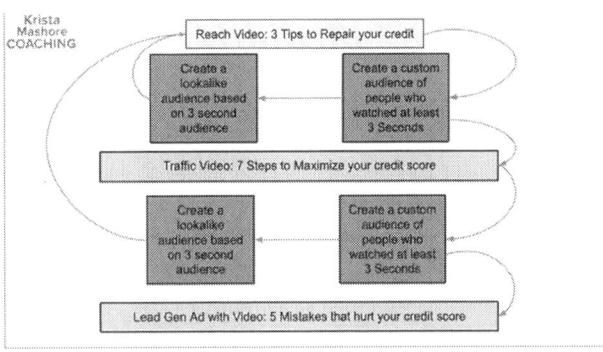

These are examples of retargeting when we talk about how to properly use Facebook on page 18-19.

Social Media Analytics for Past Properties

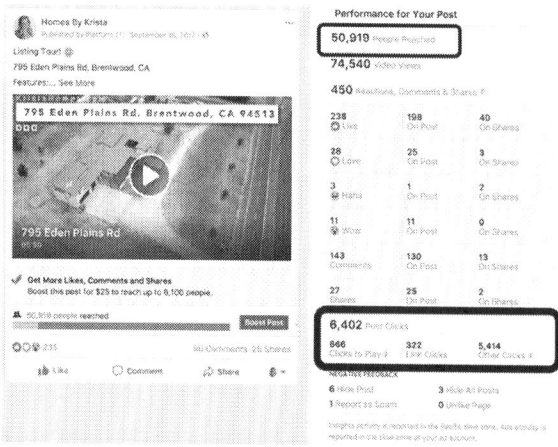

50,919 people reached means that many people saw this ad for this home! Video Views means 15 seconds or more was watched. 74,540 people watched 15 seconds or more of this property tour video! Post clicks means the number of times people clicked to go to my website, which means 6,402 people visited my website!

The Savvy Seller

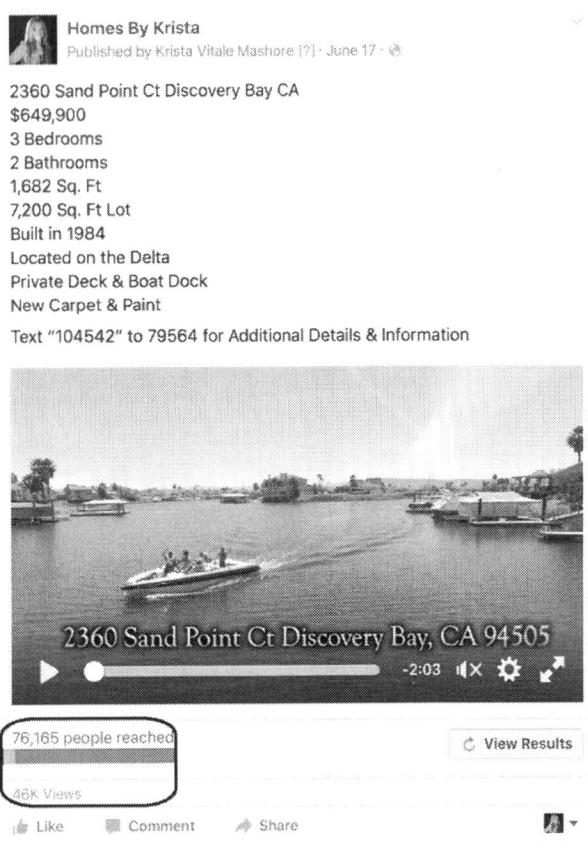

76,165 people reached means that many people saw this ad for this home!

Made in the USA
Middletown, DE
10 March 2021

35173338R00049